The "first of many",

Congratulations and Well done.

01-11-02.

LESSONS IN LOVE

Edited by

Rachael Radford

First published in Great Britain in 2002 by
ANCHOR BOOKS
Remus House,
Coltsfoot Drive,
Peterborough, PE2 9JX
Telephone (01733) 898102

HB ISBN 1 84418 032 8
SB ISBN 1 84418 033 6

FOREWORD

Yin and Yang, the two halves that make a whole. All our featured poets have taken time out to celebrate their other halves, soul mates, be they a partner, lover, sibling or best friend.

Who has been the one to hold your hand through the darkest nights and rejoice in your triumphs and pleasures?

Lessons In Love is a special collection of poems written purely from the heart - sharing the true joys of what it really is to love somebody. You are invited to enjoy the magic of love in all its many guises, along with its mixture of lust, envy, compassion and heartache that accompanies us from childhood to our adult years.

Rachael Radford
Editor

CONTENTS

TIME TO LOVE

Love can sometimes seem quite a bit of a muddle
But there's always time for a kiss and a cuddle
Beautiful things seem the same in your eyes as before
Flowers, trees, birds, animals, even the rug on the floor.
Children, grandchildren, family members and more
The throng seems to have grown with numbers galore
Your love's still there and certainly much stronger
Although life seems shorter and nights much longer.
You've had a good life and enjoyed every bit
It's definitely changing so make the most of it.

Trevor Beach

LOVE

What hand of fate took my soul from the sea
And delivered it into the hands of thee?
Out there you stood on silver sands
And beckoned me forth with outstretched hands.
And when my heart began to burn
I waited for the tides to turn
But we were stranded on the shores of time
And soon I wanted you to be mine.
Yet still in vain I looked about
I could not see being blind with doubt.
You called me but I heard no voice
I searched for escape; there was no choice
In mists of tears I hid my eyes
I covered my ears afraid of lies
I looked at the body you had caressed
And felt my heart within my breast
Could I possibly begin to dare
That if I turned you'd still be there?
Great jagged rocks continued to echo their threats
But fishermen still cast their nets
Lost though I was I took a stride
But weakness had made me need a guide
And there you were to my great relief
Although your face was lined with grief
And so it was on that vivid day
I vowed I would never run away
By your side I always want to be
In love with you and you with me.

Angela Cookson

MY THOUGHTS OF YOU

My thoughts are often just of you,
And the things together that we could do,
Arm in arm in the countryside stroll along,
Listening to the birds in song,
Watch the swallows flying at speed,
Gathering food for their chicks in need,
Having a picnic in the shade of the trees,
Wondering at the work of honey bees,
The stream would flow at a leisurely pace,
And I'd see contentment on your face,
Pour some wine and drink a toast,
To the one I dearly love the most,
See the sun set in a warm, red glow,
Then you and I we surely know,
The time has come for us to part,
We kiss adieu with a heavy heart,
Then long for the time that we can be,
Together once more just you and me,
In each other's arms in harmony.

Les Whittle

DEAR JOYCE

The sound of your voice
Winging its way across the ocean
Still lingers in my heart.
You did not need words -
The joy in your soul came bubbling through
Before the words could form!
It was infectious,
And I drew great comfort from your voice.
I miss you Joyce!

Joan Tompkins

WE ARE ONE

At the bottom of our hearts,
I feel we have a place for each other,
That's why I know we can learn to share
And learn to love one another.
At the beginning of time,
We were just dust in the darkness,
Shining from the light from the sun.
But as time goes by, I realise
We're not on the planet, we're in it,
So we are the Earth,
And we are one.

Sophie Furmage

SPECIAL LOVE

Look all around you
love is in the air.
Love of family and friends
who are always there.

A friendly face,
a shining smile.
Someone who,
will always stop for a while.

Listen to your woes
and share your every pleasure.
Such special love
is something to treasure.

Julie Brown

CUPID

When cupid fired his arrows,
He aimed them pretty straight,
He timed it to perfection,
He could have been too late!

As they travelled to their targets,
Sprinkling magic dust,
That tiny little cherub said,
'This really is a must!'

And now he's left two people,
Feeling wonderful indeed,
But they must tread quite carefully,
If they are to succeed.

He insists this special magic,
Forever - there must be,
And a lasting love so wonderful,
For all eternity.

Carol Edney

PARTING

A look, a touch, two thoughts unite;
So deep, but no one knows.
It's just within the heart of us,
As tender as a rose.

How it began, when love was born,
A care, a wish, a sigh -
We can't recall, but we just knew
Our hearts could never lie.

The years roll by, just like a dream;
Our eyes and hearts grow old.
If love was weighed, then ours would be
More than the world could hold!

How can I part with you my love?
They say your life is through.
They've told me I must say goodbye
I'll surely follow you!

I sit alone and ponder now,
And think of love gone by.
Although your life is over now
Our love will never die.

Beryl Clark

MY ONLY VALENTINE

I knew he would forget again, so different at the start,
Then it was a bunch of flowers, a chocolate covered heart,
After all these years I guess, the romance starts to cool,
I'm just a silly woman, a middle-aged old fool.

I can't sit here, there's things to do, the chores are calling me,
Washing, dusting, making beds and something for the tea,
He's been my love all through the years, always by my side,
I've never needed anything, he looks at me with pride.

So what's a card I tell myself, when love is all I've known,
He tells me when he looks at me, it's all he's ever shown,
I must not grumble, some have less, I'm happy as can be,
I'll bake a cake and make for him, a very special tea.

My hand in flour the doorbell rang, whoever can this be?
It always seems to happen, when I'm busy with the tea,
Upon the step a big bouquet, of roses crimson red,
They must be for the girl next door, to myself I said.

I took them through the kitchen, and laid them to one side,
And carried on preparing, my teatime treat surprise,
When all was done and ready, the flowers caught my eye,
On lifting them to smell their scent, the card I did espy.

Addressed to me a little card, I read through falling tears
Each rose I give to you my love, one for each missing year,
When I forgot to send a card, but darling know it's true,
I may not say it as I ought, but I always will love you.

Kathleen Townsley

A LOVE STORY

It was like something out of a novel
and Italy is where it was set.
It was almost the end of the war
when this young couple first met.

Their relationship developed into love,
they were more than happy with life.
This Englishman thought that just maybe
she would agree to be his wife.

He was welcomed into her family
who loved his gentle way.
He asked them for their daughter's hand,
which he had practised all through the day.

They were to be married in Italy,
where she became a war bride.
Then they left for England
where he showed her off with pride.

She quickly settled into her new life
and soon regarded it as home.
Obviously missing her folks a lot
who came from Naples and Rome.

They now have a grown-up family
to seal the love that they had.
But this was no story, it's real
for they are my mom and my dad.

Pauline Russell

LIFE'S LOVE

To soar above the highest cloud
in desire and love so strong
filling you with passion loud
no other love could ever long
for love and love's sweet song
the beauteous joy of total love
when hours are as passing minutes
in the heady height of love's desire
when flying high on silken skies
feeling love's consuming fire
safely secured locked in love
that love that comes but once
that caresses only youth
when all the world is instant
no time to waste on weary woes
or the fear that comes with age
you live for now not tomorrow
frittering time you only borrow
all in the pursuit of love's allure
the love that you pray each day
will succour last and so endure
throughout life's many miles
so be aware when love first bites
mind you guard it with your life
for when you secure love
all the world belongs to you
love from heaven is truly true.

K K Campbell

LOVE IS

Love is the little things your husband will do for you
                                        without being asked.
Love is the gentleness and peacefulness in which you have basked.
Love is the fights you will have and the making up supreme.
Love is thoughts of poets, and their dream.
Love is the colour of the sun, on a warm day.
Love is the garden flowers all in bright array.
Love is your pets who know they are adored.
Love is a little child, when it is feeling bored.
Love is still, a mystery of which we in turn unfold.
Love is still, a story that is here to be told.

Zoe French

All My Love Always

Just a note to tell you son,
How much you mean to me,
To tell you that I'm happy and
How very proud I'll be.

To see you getting married,
Will fill me full of pride,
Especially when I see you,
With your new wife by your side.

We've shared some special memories,
Some good and some quite sad,
Especially in the days,
When we were left without your dad.

A lengthy operation and facing life anew,
You helped me and gave strength to me,
You helped me see it through.

Especially in those times,
You were a great support to me
And I'll be forever grateful,
For the love you showed to me.

From being small
You've cared for me,
Just like I've cared for you,
So this is why I'm sending,
All my love to you.

I hope that you'll be happy,
In the future with your bride,
With good luck, good health,
And lots of love to keep you satisfied.

Kathleen South

FIRST LOVE, FIRST KISS

Ever since the first time I gazed upon your face
Your smile held my heart in a warm embrace.
Look into my eyes and they will reveal
Just how deeply about you I feel.
My love for you I can no longer conceal.

As you lean closer our lips finally meet,
So close I can feel your body heat.
The world seems out of place as my pulse begins to race.
My spirits start to soar, until you break away.
Leaving my lips crying out for more.

Angela Henderson

MOST FELT, LEAST UNDERSTOOD

Love, a most felt but least understood feeling,
Craves care in all degrees with which we're dealing.
An example is an ex-girlfriend's mother,
Although it could quite well be someone other.
Long after her young daughter to me had cooled,
One mother protested at being so ruled.
'You never come to see us now,' she complained,
A truth which was easier said than explained.
Alone together at the theatre just once,
With this older partner I'd felt a mute dunce.
Never having been a teenager before,
I didn't know such a state was nat'ral law.
We had gone to see The Winslow Boy, a play
Which showed youth must be seen to choose the right way.
Morally uplifted but confused inside,
I decided the friendship should be denied.
But with better control of feelings and fact,
That warm link should have been saved with care and tact.

Allan Bula

UNTITLED

Those who cry the most tears don't feel the most pain
Crocodile tears accomplish self gain
Tears of frustration often say
I am going to have my way
Tears for love's refrain
Many are cried in vain
Tears of happiness when love blooms again
Tears for a loved one passed away
In loving memory will forever stay
Tears of laughter and joy
On the arrival of a baby girl or boy
A mother's tears when her young leave the nest
May your life with sunshine be blessed
We learn from experience through the years
Some pain is too deep for tears.

Sheila Burke

LOST LOVE

Yesterday was all we had.
Those hours of love's content
Still linger on, in memory clad,
With tender words well meant.

No soaring birds will ever sing
As sweet as they did then.
Nor will the first green buds of spring
Speak to my heart again.

The leaves fall soft and gentle now,
As autumn runs its course.
So bleak and barren is the bough
That echoes my remorse.

Faded our love like summer flowers,
Heavy my heart and sad,
I thought tomorrow would be ours,
But yesterday was all we had.

Dorothy A Murphy

IN DREAMS

In dreams last night I travelled far
Across the seas to where you are.
A distant land, some time gone by,
What happened to us, you and I?

Beside blue waters, on golden sand,
We strolled together, hand in hand.
Sunshine blazed from a cloudless sky,
And we swore our love would never die.

If only I could reach you now,
See you, touch you, tell you how,
My life's been good but lonely too -
I still wake each morning missing you.

Sue Murray

If They Said . . .

Choose a man to share your life
Choose a man and be his wife,
Who would it be I hear them ask
And would it be an easy task?

Would he be a handsome brute?
Someone cuddly and very cute?
Would he have loads of money?
Would he sometimes call me Honey?

Would he take me on a cruise?
Give me anything I choose?
Give me lots of fancy things?
Give me shiny diamond rings?

No -
The man I'd choose to share my life
Is the man who chose me to be his wife,
The man who loves me strong and true
My darling Michael, that man is you.

Mary Elliott

LIGHT OF MY LIFE

Looking back I know just when
This love affair of ours began,
I remember every detail
Your smile, your touch, that haunting look,
You became my soul, my spirit,
My every day and joy within it,
My very existence is just for you
My sunrise and setting sun.

Walking hand in hand
Lost in a world of our own making,
Every day a new beginning
Made for us just for the taking,
Can't we stop the sands of time
For this love of yours and mine?

The candle of life burns so bright
Lighting every step we take
Making sure we do not stumble
Making sure we know the way,
The flickering flame repels the darkness
When sometimes it tries to creep in
Its long slender tendrils of dark, dancing shadows
Angry because it's kept at bay.

I will always be here,
I will always be near,
You will feel my love hold you,
You will hear my heart tell you,
I love you my darling,
I love you.

Mary Neill

PRECIOUS LOVE

To be gifted with love,
Is a treasure to hold,
Enjoy every moment,
And treat it like gold,
It enhances your life,
Makes easier your troubles,
Caring and sharing,
Think of each other with love, every time,
And never let go as the years entwine.

Sylvia Farr

SUMMER LOVE

I sat alone on golden sand, the sun shone high above,
The gentle waves lapped on the shore, where is my summer love?
I know that he will come to me, I feel that he is near,
Then from the blue and silver waves, my lover does appear.

I gazed into his dark brown eyes, he gently stroked my hair,
Then drew me close against his chest, still wet, I did not care.
Warm tears filled my eyes and then ran softly down my cheek,
So warm and tender was his kiss, I found I could not speak.

We sat and watched the sun go down, across the golden sea,
I laid my head against his chest, his strong arms holding me.
As darkness fell, a silver moon rose above so high
It touched the beach, kissed the sea, and lit the starry sky.

Along the silver moonlit shore, together, hand in hand
We strolled along in silence leaving footprints in the sand.
We lay down in the soft, warm sand, and watched the stars above,
That night upon the silver sand we made such precious love.

I woke to find myself alone, whilst seagulls wheeled above,
While golden sunrise lit the sky, wept for my summer love.
I knew he'd have to leave me, knew it couldn't last,
Once again we would be separated by the past.

Long ago, this man I love, was taken from my life,
Here upon this very beach, begged me to be his wife.
We kissed and pledged eternal love, he ran towards the sea,
And jumped into the cold cruel waves, and never came back to me.

Now every year, this very day, he does come back to me,
To make love in the soft warm sand, then returns to the cold, cruel sea.

Marisa Greenaway

TODAY IS THE FIRST DAY OF THE REST OF MY LIFE

Today something changed in my life
Because I found the girl of my dreams,
I watch her walk by with a special look in her eye
I wonder what that look means?

Should I ask her out, what will she say?
Will she say yes?
Could she look at me that way?

When we are apart
I wonder why,
Inside I would cry.

I tear apart
When you are not near
Because I fear
That you don't hear the sound of my heart.

Today something changed in my life
I asked the girl of my dreams to be my wife
Will she be mine until the end of time?

Today is the first day of the rest of my life.

Jonathan Halls

LOVE

Today I can write some happy lines,
Because you love me and I love you,
Every day is a new beginning,
And the love in your eyes is always new.

With someone who adores you,
You feel happy all the time,
Just gazing in each other's eyes,
And knowing that you're mine.

The touch of your hand is strong, yet gentle,
And it makes me feel warm inside,
Just looking at you across the room,
Makes me glow with pride.

Nina Solon (17)

MY WORLD IS BREAKING

My world is breaking
I just can't go on without you in my life
So let's tell people about you
Let's just get it out in the open.

No more secrets
No more sorrow
So let's tell people tomorrow.

I don't want to share you
I want everyone to know you're mine
I hope to spend my life with you
Until the end of time.

No more secrets
No more sorrow
Let's tell people tomorrow.

Your lovely golden hair
Floating in mid air
Your eyes melt me,
Your lips tease me.

No more secrets
No more sorrow
Let's tell people tomorrow.

When I think about you
Every night, every day,
My love for you grows stronger
In every way.

No more secrets
No more sorrow
Let's tell people tomorrow.

Lucy Chance

INFIDELITY

As moonbeams kiss . . . the starry night
And lighting up the beach . . . so bright
Two lovers meet . . . just holding hands
Beside a palm . . . on silver sands.

They're talking still . . . but holding tight
And gently kissing . . . oh so light
On lips as red . . . as cherry wine
Just standing there . . . and taking time.

Then walking . . . on with meeting eyes
And heaving breasts . . . and gentle sighs
With smiles and laughs . . . with mixed emotions
And visions of their . . . such deep devotions.

As midnight breezes . . . chill the air
That's blowing through . . . her golden hair
They stop again . . . still holding tight
And kissing in . . . the pale moonlight.

Then kneeling down . . . still hand in hand
She slowly lays back . . . in the sand
And closing eyes . . . she hopes to see
Her long awaited . . . ecstasy.

And as those dark clouds . . . sail on by
And blotting out . . . the silver sky
Both lips meet . . . and kiss so tight
Without the realms of . . . darkest night.

Their souls are open . . . hearts laid bare
Romantic echoes . . . fill the air
As passion rises . . . then soon gone
But holding arms . . . still lingers on.

Still as time . . . the moment goes
Resting still . . . in sweet repose
But oh what tangled web . . . they weave
They cannot stay . . . so they must leave.

Returning to . . . their former life

As someone's husband . . . and someone's wife.

R E Weedall

KEYS

Turn the key to unlock the door
Unlock your feelings to be free.

Keys keep things safe,
Keys to your heart,
Keys to your life,
Keys to your door.

Turn the key to unlock the door
Unlock your feelings to be free.

If you can't talk,
You're locked inside,
Signs open minds
And set us free.

Turn the key to unlock the door
Unlock your feelings to be free.

When you're in love,
You swap your keys,
You hold mine
And I hold yours.

Turn the key to unlock my heart,
Unlock your feelings to be free.

Secrets and lies,
Lock up your heart,
In a prison,
In the dark.

Turn the key to unlock the door
Unlock your feelings to be free.

Jenny Duff

LOVE

Love is magical
Love can make a plain person beautiful
Love can make one feel wonderful
In the eyes a warm and tender glow
There is a new spring in the step
Love brings a brand new confidence
And a joy to be alive.
The whole world appears to be on your side
Loving and being loved in return
That dizzy dancing feeling in your heart
May that love eternally burn.

The love in your life is gone
Now you are again on your own
All your dearest dreams have melted
Like a beautiful flower that's wilted.
No more the head in the clouds
The clouds are now filled with rain.
The heart is heavy, the tears and the anguish
And oh the hurt, oh God how it hurts,
With such exquisite pain
Like a moth in the flame.
With all your heart and being
You wish that they were here
To heal the hurts and dry the tears
And loving you again.

Sue Bownass

ENIGMA

At times, when far apart we've been,
I've felt my heart send waves of love
Towards your lonely life. I've seen,
In dreams, you lift your head above
The ruins that were yesteryear.
Sensing my love and gentleness
I've known that, somehow, all your fear
Has vanished with your loneliness.
To me you were so very dear,
So far, my darling, yet so near.

And now our dreams, my precious one,
Are in reality at last.
Together every deed is done,
Forgotten is the fading past.
Tempestuous as lovers are,
We are so near and yet so far.

Joy Atkins

LOVE IS IN THE AIR

The white button-down shirts and loud pin-up girl neckties
Sharp Hepworth gabardine suiting with metal zip trouser flies
Blood-soaked paper stuck faces from last minute shaves
Sleek Silvikrinned Tony Curtis D A's and setting lotion waves.

That funny sad poignancy of early 1950's romancing
With inebriated approaches in end of evening Palais de Dances
The next night rendezvous in smoke choking saloon bars
And later clumsy kiss copying of smooth Hollywood film stars.

The self-conscious proclamations of eternal devotion
From folded raincoat carrying youths embarrassed by emotion
The white cardigan clad girls on shadowy street corners
Defiantly defending their virtue with the ferocity of jaguars.

The Sunday tea summons from her mistrustful mother
To be settee wedged with her father and fidgety young brother
Inquisition like questions about parents and intentions
The sudden suspicion this could be the start of a life of detention.

The dire attempts at conversation and long boring tales
And slight twinge of disappointment as all efforts to impress fail
That funny look from her mother when you thank her for tea
And her eager slam of the back door as you walk away to be free.

The smirks from your mates when they find out that it's over
Spiteful claims from old girlfriends that you were always a loser
The rejected temptation to play the poor broken-hearted
Before dressing yourself up, and heading back where it all started.

Tom Eadie

FINDING LOVE

I've had all the glory,
Coupled with pain,
Found new forms of love that drove me insane.

Feelings twisted beyond despair,
In my search for a maiden ever so fair.
An epic journey with tales to tell,
Exciting experiences which make my heart swell.

Of all the women I've known and loved,
None has taken me to that level above,
I would throw away all and everything that I am,
Only to that special woman who can complete me as a man.

I'll carry on and keep searching in hope that I'll find,
That angel to cherish in this heart of mine.
If I fail in all that I do,
At least I touched some hearts that were stale and blue.

To all the new friends I met on the way,
Thanks for being around to brighten my days,
The fun, the laughs and companionship I've had,
Makes life worth living and makes me feel glad.

If I should fail in my epic quest,
Know that I tried my very best.
Should I succeed and to the woman that takes my hand,
I'll promise to be that complete man.

The morale of this story and what I'm really trying to say,
Life is funny but sweet in its own kind of way.

David Wong

ROMANCE?
(For my partner)

Love is quite a good selling technique.
Pining away as I do all week
For some boy or another
Or even my brother.

There's someone called George Michael
Who's used love in his music to sell
Says 'True love asks for nothing'
I am ashamed!
I'm always asking for stuff.

Love can make you feel a bit rough
Lovesick in or out of it.
Getting dumped being particularly nasty.

But when it's good, it's good, so good
Good as the Grim Reaper in his hood
Taking us from here
Suffering terrible fear
But good because then there may be Heaven
What more is romance?

Love is just a word, but more than a word
It needs action to prove it.
Romance could be groovy.
Marriage tempting although absurd.
I'd like lots of presents please.

Lucy Taylor

PERFECT PEACE

After the passion's spent,
The ecstasy that Heaven sent,
I lie in sweet content,
And I sleep in perfect peace,

Lost and locked in nakedness,
You lay your head upon my chest,
My name's a whisper on your breath,
And I sleep in perfect peace,

You gave your love to me,
Sweet sensuality,
Anticipation not dismayed,
Love's a game,
And how we played,

Then I wake holding you near,
Thanking God that you're still here,
Happiness becomes a tear,
That falls upon your skin,
Then my lips take up this dew,
I love the very taste of you,
Love's a dream we fell into,
And I sleep in perfect peace,

An angel's wings have lifted me,
Up to serenity.
Heaven's real I can see,
It's a place called you and me,

After the passion's spent,
The ecstasy that Heaven sent,
I lie in sweet content,
And I sleep in perfect peace.

A Heart

UNTITLED

If you ever falter or start to sway
Think of tomorrow, not today
Never shall you find a better lover
Deeper than known between sister and brother
A token of which your parents gave
One to cherish, one that can stay
If patience is needed to rekindle your heart
Remember tomorrow how life was apart
Relieve yourself of this burden of fear
The fear that some day our love will disappear
Because just as the sun returns each day
Our love, my friend, is here to stay . . .

Ajay

BROKEN PROMISE

I never thought you could leave me
I thought you would always stay
You promised me eternity
To love, honour and obey.

How easy it was for you to go
To break the ties that bind
Off to a new life of adventure
Why are you always on my mind?

I was completely addicted to you
You always came first
You were my wine, I need a drink
Only you can satisfy my thirst.

'Take me back,' you pleaded
But I could never forgive the pain
I told you to go back to her
Everyone said I was insane.

They say time will heal the hurt
I suppose in a way that is true
I will spend the rest of my life alone
So in love with you.

Linda Lawton

MY RAINBOW

I have an ache within my heart that will never leave.
Every day the storm clouds loom, I feel I have to grieve.
I found a rainbow one dull day and glimpsed its pot of gold,
but sadly as I grew closer, I couldn't grab a hold.
I wanted the gold so badly, I'd go to any length,
but the constant struggle to reach it took away my strength.
I'd go to bed each evening and dream the gold was mine,
I woke with the reality that my water was not wine.
The struggle to cope left me feeling all alone,
my gold that once glistened now turned to stone.
I wanted so much to see my rainbow through the clouds of rain,
and to find my pot of gold that would make me whole again.

Jackie Washington

THE SWOON

That often scorned, derided description
about the bygone, Victorian condition
at a dance, a ball, so formal, so polite,
where gentlemen and ladies, danced a summer's night.

When everything, tradition, propriety and permission
brought about excitement, or frowns, or condescension,
to accommodate the rigid, structure of society,
allowances to court, beneath the eyes of their majesty.

The ladies, the mothers, of recently brought-out debutante,
regarded their duties as chaperones, a serious response
to, as yet, unawoken, realisation, of love, a token
of intention to claim and capture, this age-old match, invention.

The god of love, it's true, invented love and romance
as the precursor to this intention, for families, announce
the age of freedom to courtship, in the tradition
from the earliest, historical setting, an exhibition.

When a man had captured the whole-hearted admiration
from a young, escorted and closely chaperoned, new generation
and his intentions, so honourable, so true,
had need to bring about her capitulation, was proven, by a swoon.

This was the final testament to his capture
for upon her feet, her awakening, the rapture,
had made him her slave, it was the tradition
to the legally arrived-at courtship condition.

Nota bene. This actual falling asleep, has yet to be properly
investigated by scientists, who, when they discover, in reality,
the brain changes, will see, marriages have need of this necessity.

Gerasim

FOR MY LOVE

Recall the point of confluence,
When we kissed the very first time.
And our mutual influence,
As we reach such pure heights sublime.
In our river's powerful surge,
It is such a holy feeling,
As we respond to ev'ry urge,
Bringing us sexual healing,
Sharing profound intimacy,
When holding each other so tight.
Experiencing ecstasy,
Feeling at peace and safe at night,
We kiss and dry each other's tears,
When in each other's arms we lay,
Sharing deepest secrets and fears,
As desolation melts way.
It's so good to have each other,
My dear 'Huggie' and your 'Poppet',
In a love that does not smother,
But makes our endorphins rocket!

Winifred Rickard

REJECTION

My heart is heavy, painful and sad,
A trouble within me growing fast.
Pulling at every thought I have,
Why can't he love me,
Be gentle and glad?

My eyes see with sorrow
My ears hear with pain
The hardness in his voice as he calls my name.
The words he forms are hard and rough
The dissatisfaction is plain enough.

I am the young girl he once used to love
Now I am the woman he can't bear to touch
I am the woman he used to bed
Now I am old and I will never wed.

Anne Dunkerley

THE SMILE

Oh, I have seen the smile upon your face,
A beautiful smile, when you and I embraced,
You clung to me, as I did you,
We snoozed together, just you and I,
All too soon, time slipped by,
You had nothing particular to do,
In the same situation I was too,
Me, the old and you, the new,
Your little hand gripped the finger of mine,
We stayed like that for quite some time,
The picture of love and innocence,
Adorned your lovely smile,
Making all about you, wonderful and worthwhile,
Our loving encounter, is with me today,
As I scroll this poem in my usual way,
Thinking of the day when you joined planet Earth,
You brought much happiness and sounds of mirth,
For you, our granddaughter,
With your whole life before you,
We need some time, to hug and adore you,
You smiled even more when I whispered your name,
No look of annoyance, or look of disdain,
The magic of life, is a wonderment to me,
I've had years of experience, so I know you see!
Looking upon you, it came as no surprise,
When tears of happiness dampened my eyes,
Nothing upon Earth could better your smile,
I'll just stay here and linger a while.
Soon, no doubt, we will have to part,
I have this picture of you, next to my heart.

John H Israel

OUR FIRST KISS

The magic moment has to be,
which sticks out in my memory
is of our first most gentle kiss,
as I sit and reminisce.

We stood close to say goodbye
when the time had just flown by.
We looked into each other's eyes,
So when we touched it was no surprise.

Four hours earlier we had never met,
but since then I have not one regret.
I think of the feeling of ecstasy
with my sweet Karen kissing me.

Never the excitement felt before
for me now as I recall.
She gives me her love so supreme,
darling Karen, the girl of my dreams.

Mike Wetson

MAKING MY DAY

I love to wake each morning and to find you waiting there
I love to watch you rise each day and brush away my cares
You greet each day with brightness that only you can do
And I am very happy to take my warmth from you.

You ask for nothing in return yet give so much to me
You are my feel-good factor and every day I see
That I can't live without you, I need your guiding light
This overpowering need is with me day and night.

The days that you are missing I just can't get things right
With banks of cloud up in the sky I try with all my might
To visualise you back again and hope that you'll take care
And I will wake tomorrow and find you waiting there.

You cast an evening shadow and an evening breeze may blow
But no one in this whole wide world could ever love you so
You are my inspiration and without you I would die
So when I draw the curtains back I need you in my sky.

Now if you're still confused by my passion or my love
When you wake in the morning take a lingering look above
And you will see (well, hopefully) what this is all about
And if it's not, it won't be long before the sun is out.

Jackie Davies

FIRST ENCOUNTER

We met in spring, one lovely day
When first you smiled at me
You lingered, and I hoped you'd stay,
I just knew it had to be.

You shyly offered me your hand
My own felt right within it
And from then on it felt so grand
Each and ev'ry minute.

We stood and watched the setting sun
The day had gone so fast
It was the day we set upon
Life's course of love to last.

Joan Fletcher

IT'S THAT . . .

That smile,
that look,
that touch,
that face.
Forever a part of me
you will be.
That song
that smiling day
that closeness
that 'let's pretend'.
On our own, just you and me
together forever, remembering:
that smile,
that look,
that touch,
that face
that magic . . .

Kathy O'Connor

LOVE ANEW

Love anew is so divine,
Like sparkling rose petal wine.
Like sunshine softly burning in my heart!

You are the key to the door of all my dreams.
With you my love anew
I feel that I could touch the moon,

And while I was reaching for the moon I'd catch
Some stars and give them to you!
O' my love anew.

For you are the fire that lights my sky
O love anew is so divine!
Like sparkling rose petal wine.

Viv Eckett

I Feel It

I feel it, it's sending my mind a'reeling,
I feel it, it's so grand and revealing,
I feel it, it's from my head to my toes,
I feel it, it's a tingling in my nose.
I feel it, it's sending shivers down my spine,
I feel it, it's a feeling just fine,
I feel it, it's like walking on air,
I feel it, it's knowing that I care,
I feel it, it's more than just an attraction,
I feel it, it brings a great satisfaction,
It is . . . Love that I am feeling,
        coursing through my very being.
And now . . .
        My heart is full to the brim, it's true
        all because, my love of *you* . . .

Bernice Sharpe

To My Dearest Lesley

Love Looks

Love looks with the mind not just with the eyes
As the real beauty exists inside
From outside I look so deep within
As beauty also exists beneath your skin

People look but do not see
The real beauty that's inside of thee
They merely look and see a shell
But don't look deep inside as well

I look at you and see so much
To feel your soft and tender touch
To let me know this is no dream
That you really are my Beauty Queen

From the first time that we agreed to meet
I knew your beauty was not just skin deep
So I hope it comes as no surprise
That I looked with my mind, not just with my eyes.

All my love to you always Honey

Pete xxx

Pete Hazell

COMMITTED

Shall I compare thee to a winter's day?
Thou art more cold and unforgiving too.
Rough winds are more inviting, cold as clay.
Refrigeration, could apply to you,
In Arctic circles bears have warmer climes.

Eskimos and Lapps on icy plains rejoice
I would enjoy some warmer-hearted times,
Some feeling, even tenderness of voice.

You were once sweet and tender, in times past
This awful illness, not your fault it's true,
But, oh how long is this sentence to last?
How long can I be faithful, dear, to you?

In sickness and in health we made a vow.
So, forever, I'm committed to you now.

Marjorie Grant

A GARDEN OF EDEN

You're the most beautiful woman I have ever seen.
You're lovelier than the dawn and the sunset combined.
You have smashed the citadel of my carefully guarded heart
With one innocent look, so tender, refined.

You're like a bright clear light in my darkness.
Your eyes like the glow of a candle flame.
You make all around me seem rich with colour
And fragrant with scent, no sense of shame.

I would walk through fire just to be beside you
And to show you the passion I feel from within.
If this is a dream then I don't want to know it,
As I breathe in the fragrance of your delicate skin.

Shadows whisper between us like gentle voices,
Drawing us closer and closer still.
Your lips brush mine with extraordinary tenderness,
Gently warming my heart with the thrill.

Excruciating pleasure rolling right through us,
In wave after consuming wave.
As I kissed you again in tender reverence.
Accepting the solace that you freely gave.

No amount of money, skill or persuasion,
Can buy the heart or soul of a woman or man.
We freed each other with our endless love,
As if it was all in some master plan.

A place where we gave our hearts to each other.
A Garden of Eden just for we two.
Euphoric dreams of being together,
With you loving me and me loving you.

M J Plummer

SILENT VIGIL

You hold me in your gentle arms
Whilst silent vigil keeping
I feel your warm and tender love
Even as I'm sleeping

And when I awake you're always there
Constantly by my side
Your love and strength will see me through
Each day till eventide

So, my love, it will always be
Until our time on Earth is over
Then, in Heaven, you and I
Our love we'll re-discover.

Valerie McKinley

(GAZZA) 'I NEEDED YOU'

I was battered and bruised
I was physically used,
Even my mind was mentally abused!
I hated myself, for what I'd become
So I took my boy and went home to my mum!

To exist again, I never did think
To feel pretty and seem like a woman,
But then I met you, from the start, yes, I knew,
One day I would finally be married to you!

You gave me and give me the love that I need
I wake in the morning, can smile,
We now have a daughter, and you have my son,
Together forever, our family is one.

We'll be married in July
I know that we'll both cry,
But my tears are my heartbeats for you,
Cos without you my Gazza
I know I would be
Plodding along and not this happy!

Michelle Hinchcliffe

EYES ACROSS THE ROOM

How many long years have now gone by since first they shared
                                                    that dream,
Of life full of wondrous plans to take them to where joy belongs?
Together they made memories, bred in their rapture supreme.
Suddenly it all collapsed and their rights turned into their wrongs.
Now they are at the party, will they go to the wild extreme,
To meet in a hate explosion and fight like hammer and tongs?
She turned her head, he looked up, who could tell what would their
                                                    fate deem?
Their eyes met across the room and the breezes whispered love songs.

W Hunt-Vincent

AT AN END

Last night in bed, I did cry
I felt very sad, I cannot lie
For you and me, are no longer
Because our love will never grow stronger.

Maybe, perhaps, this is the end
That's why this poem, to you I send
I know you say, you still love me
But, to your heart, I have no key.

All I want is you and I
But I think we live a lie
It is easy to think that we are fine
But between love and hate, is a fine line.

I go to work and think of you
I really wish you'd think of me too
Not because I say you ought
And not because we've always fought.

But, because you want to come home
 So after nine we can be alone
To talk and laugh about our day
To say everything will be OK.

Just the little things in my life
I know you think I'm just your wife
I want you to be interested in me
But I think, deep down, you want to be free.

Over the last few months, it has got worse
I'm beginning to think I live under a curse
All I want is a happy life
I never mean to cause you strife.

Every night I lie next to you
Wishing you would love me too
But you turn away and are so cold
You don't care anymore, or so I'm told.

Julie Livett

LOVE ME

Love me for what I am or leave me for what I'm not
Don't judge me for what I am or what I haven't got
I don't want to change you, please don't try to change me
Why can't we be ourselves and just let it be?
You loved me in the beginning so why should I be made to change?
Being something that I'm not can't be pulled off forever and feels
so very strange.
Or was I in the beginning just some passing fantasy
That you felt you had to have, and didn't even want the real me?
If this is true and, God, I hope that it is not
Then you're the one missing out on all that I have got
I know how to love, I think I've been there before
Yet what I have to give seems never enough, so I keep giving
more and more.
But in the end I found out what I was really wasn't me
And I turned into something that I didn't ever want to be
So I've come back to the person I really am and know
And find I'm better off not being somebody's whim or side show
So if you're looking for someone who will give themselves completely
Then you've made the right choice and all I ask is . . . love me.

Raymond E Buchanan

On The Night You Said You Loved Me

I wish that I could walk on ice
Cos you wouldn't have to ask me twice
To run to the sunset, you and me
Live ever after happily

Take me to Never-Never Land
Constantly holding my hand
Lead me to where sunset lies
To the forest where fairies fly

Show me Heaven don't let me go
Bathe with me where waters flow
Stand with me on the cliff side
Swimming fishes in the turning tide

Whisper softly in my ear
Words for only me to hear
Take my heart and hold on tight
Promise to keep me warm in the night

Will you set up home far away
Look out for me as from today
Believe in things I want to do
Have piece of mind and stay true

Can you catch me a falling star?
Will you run to me no matter how far?
Can you plant that seed in the earth
A new life will come after the birth

Come lay beside me on the sand
Spontaneous things are never planned
The moonlight will surely be
On the night you said you loved me.

Neil Webber

MY FEELINGS EXPLAINED

You came into my life - yes, just like that,
Whenever I saw you I felt like a prat.
You came into my life - but with you came pain,
You sent electric pulses to my brain.
Whenever you spoke I felt all dizzy,
My heart felt light and my stomach fizzy.

It wasn't liking, but it wasn't love,
It gave me a feeling of high - like floating above.
I can't explain it - it was too complex,
Just like hormones playing with the opposite sex.
A silly feeling that gives you a rush,
All it was, was a stupid crush.

It hurt so much, I knew it had to stop.
I felt as though my head would 'pop'.
Too many strange emotions, what'll I do?
The answer's simple, stop liking you!
That should work - at least I'll give it a try,
And if it doesn't, sure I can always lie!

A few months on and all's a mess,
My feelings are still strong and I want to confess,
To tell you of my love, to see what you think,
In hope that you'll save me and pull me back from the brink.
Because being without you is driving me insane,
And causing my heart a great deal of pain.

Ciara McBrien

CHANGE

Every single sleepless night
they dreamed their lives away.
So close, yet so far apart.
He alive as electric wire;
She as dead as dry wood.
Death without a coffin.
A coffin without a corpse.
Both gazing at the moon
playing 'hide go seek'
between the runaway clouds
while making room for the
early morning burglar to
break and enter.
They welcome the sight of
the spidery sun stretching
its golden legs and blinding
them out of bed.
That change had changed everything.
He wrestled with an RC conscience while she
realised oranges weren't the only fruit.
The straws they were both clutching at
spelt out one word, celibacy, and there
was no turning back.

Francis Hughes

THREE YEARS AGO

Three years ago I lost my head
I let you into my heart and bed
I gave you loving you just couldn't handle
You snuffed it out like you would a candle
You gave me dreams and promises and hope
And lies enough to make me choke!
I gave you trust as a friend
I should have known that it was all pretend
You used me time after time
And that wasn't your only crime
You went from my bed to hers and back again
And through it all I was expected to stay sane
I was expected to prop you upright
Trusting your words with blinkered sight
Don't do this. Don't do that. Don't be like her.
Your rules ruffled my fur
I couldn't hate you or even grieve
I wasn't allowed any relief
Expected always to carry on
Where are you now my strength is gone?
And so here we are
Enemies at love and war
Where will we be?
I wish that I could see.

Teresa Whaley

PAPA LUIGI

Dry your eyes and finish your tea,
there's only a heartbeat
between you and me,
there's only a whisper,
a sunset, a dawn,
you've been in my heart
since the day you were born.

I'll never desert you,
I'll never be far,
just reach out for me
and I'll be where you are.

I'll always be with you,
watch over you all,
be there when you stand
and there when you fall.

I'll cherish your laughter
and wince at your tears,
my love won't diminish
through death or through years,
I'm with you, I love you,
beside you I'll stay,
until our reunion in Heaven one day.

Catherine Thornton

DRINKING

I'm drinking again to drown my sorrows,
My heartache cries, I'm dreading tomorrow.

I swear never again, but I'm easily led,
You see it's the loneliness I dread.

I hate the nights with the fading light,
But a bottle of booze becomes my favourite sight.

I wake with a thirst and it's time for my first,
I've a fear inside, that I'll drink till I burst.

I'm drinking to forget, that's why I'm upset,
The love of my life, my sweetheart has left.

She left me in pain, I'm no longer the same,
I feel so ashamed but who can I blame?

I'm drowning my sorrows,
Dreading tomorrow.

David Townend

DAYDREAM

You watch him float through your mind
And you realise that he was only trying to be kind
You watch him through lands of pleasure
And know that your dreams could never measure
It's like going into a coma but you can still see the light
You think that you won't go on unless you have your right
You can see that he has been in pain and has got the scars
You wish you could help but every time you see him you
                                        feel he is put behind bars
You even ask him to stay your friend
But you realise that this is the end
You feel your heart will always be rejected
And it will never be accepted
You feel this could only be the end
As you see the light around that final bend.

H McCurry

LAUGH

The day bored, the work overcast
Until some colleague makes a witty quip.
She looks up, thinking other thoughts, then registers
And laughs, in long uncontrollable ripples of mirth.
Then memories smile across her face.
Her laugh, the first thing he'd noticed about her,
Heard again in the background of an answerphone message
When he'd called her number, scrawled on his hand.
He wished he might, one day, be able to make her laugh like that.

How strange to think of those early days
Still discovering one another.

The game mud-covered, the team lost
Until he sits, heaves off boots, discards socks
Then pauses, staring, with a grin he cannot lose.
She likes my feet, he thinks, recalling
The day she'd discovered his feet,
Delight shrieking from her eyes,
Declaring she'd thought all men's feet horrid
Until discovering these. Nice feet.
He had nice feet. The lost team wonders at his grin.

How strange to think how little the things
That keep us in each other's thoughts all day,
How very little the things,
That remind us of something so very great as this.

Paula Holt

NOW DO YOU BELIEVE IN LOVE?

You're:
Shipwrecked, on an island,
Surrounded with nothing but sea,
All that you know,
Is there's nowhere to go,
But home is where you'd like to be.
Now do you believe in love?

You're:
Sat with your partner at midnight,
You've just finished sharing your heart,
What happens now.
Is you argue somehow,
And your partner and you fall apart.
Now do you believe in love?

Tambi Maple

A LETTER TO MY BELOVED

I often think of that day at school when we were only seven,
As our eyes met across the room, I thought I was in Heaven.
I fell in love with you that day and as the time has passed,
Our feelings for each other were surely meant to last.
We both have such a lot to give and get a lot of pleasures,
From the family we have produced, our very special treasures.
Now though we are still Mum and Dad, we are Nan and Grandpa too.
Our grandchildren bring us great joy and give us lots to do.
So as I look across the room, I thank God for my life,
But most of all I thank you, dear, for making me your wife.

Eileen Bullard

LOVE IS

Love is being
Love is seeing
All wrapped up in you.

Love is caring
Love is sharing
Every dream with you.

Love is painful
Love is shameful
Not when I'm with you.

Love is now
Love is wow
Cuddling up with you.

Love is blending
Love is spending
All my time with you.

Tessa Winston

FORGIVEN

It's easy to forget the hurt we feel,
And think of a life that is not real,
But the pain of reality is so strong,
And I cannot forget what you did wrong.

Life's too short, some people say,
Let's start afresh with the new day.
The love I have for you outshines the pain,
Like the sun burning off the drops of rain.

Get closer and you will see,
How to understand the passion in me.
I've forgotten all about the past
'Cause my love for you is so vast.

Annabelle Lilly

RED

Passion. Love. Warmth
Together we were, cosy in bed,
You loved me, you said.

Danger. Crime. Lipstick
You liar, you cheat. My heart turns to lead.
Warning. Fire. Rage
The happiness we had, you ruined instead.
Anger. Blood. Pain

The love we had. Now is dead.
Staining. Rose. Stop.

Kathryn West

OUR GOLDEN WEDDING DAY

Is it really fifty years my love
Since our precious wedding day,
When you promised to be mine, my love,
Until our dying day?

It seems like only yesterday,
And yet, it seems forever,
We stood before the altar and,
I vowed to leave you never.

The years have flown, our love has grown,
No one could us sever,
God grant that we will always see
Life's journey through, together.

Madge Goodman

Us

I understand that you find it hard
To show me exactly how you feel,
It's easy to say the words 'I love you',
But showing it is what makes it real.

I really don't like it when we argue,
But I know you'll probably agree,
Being nice all the time isn't easy,
Especially with someone like me.

Giving in isn't something that I'm good at,
Saying 'Sorry' is pretty difficult too,
When you love someone as much as I love you,
That's the only right thing to do.

Still I don't think you realise,
The things I am willing to do.
Just so you and I can stay together,
'Cause I know, no one's more amazing than you.

You're such a special person
I've never met anyone like you before,
I don't know what I'd do without you,
You're everything I want and more.

I really don't want anyone else,
Expecting you to trust me is wrong,
I know that it's going to take time,
But I really don't care how long.

So believe me when I say 'I love you,'
I've never meant anything more,
This might not last for eternity,
But a while longer, I'm sure.

Nicola J Horridge

SOMETHING SPECIAL

Do you remember that day when you took me
Down to the old lakeside,
When you told me to close my eyes,
And took me on a slow boat ride?

I opened them when we were moving
And a wondrous sight I did see,
None other than the fiery horizon
Waiting for you and me.

Beneath us the water glistened
Like a lake full of blue sapphires
And from that moment on we were away,
From the evil and the liars.

You told me that you loved me
That you'd take me away from here,
Away from the sorrow from the past
That was always travelling near.

I sat there speechless,
Not knowing what I could say,
But then out of nowhere, words appeared
And I knew we'd be OK.

'Everybody's got something special to them,
Something they cherish and adore,
Something they'll hold close to their hearts
And remember for evermore.

You know I've always loved you
And nothing can change that
And all my life I've hunted for something special
But I think that I've found it at last.

Little did I realise,
That it's been here all the time,
That you're my something special
And I'm lucky that you're mine.'

And with that we sailed away,
Off into the night,
Kissing underneath the stars
And holding each other tight.

Gemma King

MIKE

You've got blue eyes
that melt my heart,
I'll love you always
don't let us part.

The more I see you
my heart thumps wildly,
then you smile
at me so kindly.

You pass me by
with your friends,
you always wave
or nod your head.

I hope our friendship
never ends,
you're my heart's desire
that lights my fire.

I'll never forget
the night we kissed,
it's the part
that I miss.

The smell, the touch,
the feel of you,
my one and only Michael
I love you.

Angela Watson

LOVE FOREVER

One day, long ago,
A girl met a boy she did not know.
They got on well; they talked for hours,
They went on dates, he bought her flowers.
Now this young girl and this young boy
Had many years of blissful joy.
After many years they were still together
And had two rings that read 'Love Forever'.
They had two sons, twins, in fact,
And these two twins made a pact.
They vowed to stay forever friends
And if they fell out to make amends.
These two twins fell out never,
And had two rings that read 'Love Forever'
These two rings went down the line,
Going from couple to couple, from time to time.
Now these two rings are very, very old.
But mine still shines like it's brand new gold!

Louise Lee

MUSCLE OF LOVE

Love is a mystical thing,
It makes the heart leap and sing,
It makes it dance and it makes it prance.

It skips a beat and it pounds,
It will drop you to the ground,
The muscle of love, gift from above.

It's happening now to me,
Once before because of he,
But if I start to think, my heart sinks.

For I know down deep inside,
My feelings I have to hide,
He feels the same, I wish anyway.

The 'he' with no name.

Helen-Elaine Oliver (14)

THE POSTMAN KNOCKED ONCE

Ease me in gently to your soft arms
Once there, protect me from all life's harms
Kiss my lips softly with lips that I adore
Whisper how you will love me forever, evermore

Let your eyes find mine and we will drown in their depths
We shall hear what our hearts speak to us - to never lose our steps
But walk through life together - with never a regret
And be truly, truly thankful that we ever met

If we stop and ponder - what life was like before
Before true love came searching and knocking on our door
We cannot seem to remember - it is just a dreary haze
What a difference that 'recorded delivery' has miraculously made!

And now we await our 'special delivery'
Created from the love of you and me
So hold me a little tighter for I know it will soon come
And I am just a little afraid of becoming someone's mum!

Lorna Marlow

THE FINAL DREAM
(Dedicated to Sue Nicholson)

Now that the dreams have finally gone
I have lost you forever,
the dreams of you have left me
how do I cope without you?

There'll be no more kissing your sweet lips
and no more touching your smooth skin,
I remember the final dream
when you cried out and said 'Goodbye.'

You kissed me gently
and you held me in your arms,
your heart was beating with mine
as you said 'I love you.'

Now that the dreams are over
I will see my dream girl no more,
your eyes will never sparkle again,
and now all I will feel is pain.

Chris T Barber

In Your Arms

I turn to you in times of trouble,
To you, in times of pain,
Your kindness then grows to double,
You give me life again.

My heart then sings a happy tune
And in your arms discovers
That true love is Heaven's boon
Since Heaven blesses lovers.

On your warm breast I shed my tears
And you encompass all,
I find a ready soul that hears,
An echo to my call.

'Tis thus the cares and griefs of day
Melt as I hold you near,
My fears take wing and fly away,
You dry my shining tear.

For men are often hard and bad
And they do sometimes shatter
Things good and fair we've built or had -
To them it doesn't matter.

But you are here to ease distress
With a soft word, a charm, a smile -
An oasis in the wilderness,
You make it all worthwhile.

Emmanuel Petrakis

I THOUGHT I SAW YOUR FACE

I thought I saw your face today
Out there in the crowd
I didn't want to miss you
So I called your name out loud . . .

It was just - a 'tiny' glimpse
Of hair with reddened hue
But my heart was beating quicker now
As I thought that I'd found you . . .

At first I walked with fastened pace
As I hurried through the street
But suddenly I felt as if
I had sprung wings upon my feet . . .

I heard my voice call out again
Your name fell on deafened ears
And then as I lost sight of you
My eyes they filled with tears . . .

My heart is like a jigsaw
The missing piece is you
I want you so to fill it
Just like the way you used to do . . .

Then as I rise from slumbers deep
The dream gone now like your face
I know that there will never be
Someone to take your place . . .

For when I look around the streets
My heart still has a gaping hole
For losing you the way I did
Has taken a great toll . . .

So if I pretend that you're still here
It might take the pain away
But who am I to kid myself
I miss you more each day.

Anne E Roberts

LOVE IS ALL IT TAKES

Let life embrace me,
Allow my soul encase me.
Forgive my windswept ways,
Enjoy the hours, the minutes, the days.
Show the love I have inside,
Never from my thoughts or feelings hide.
Just show the real person I am,
Don't in front of anyone clam.
Although it's hard sometimes,
Make way for warmer climes.
The warmth will melt away the cold,
You'll be stronger and more bold.
You can hold a baby in your arms,
Turn all anxieties into calms.
Another day, another challenge to face,
But look for the better way, the brighter place.
Be of good heart, when you can do,
Try to exchange with everyone too.
Don't give way to hate,
Never go to such a lower state.
Then one day life could be,
Emotionally, psychologically and completely free.

Karen Stephens

OUR JOURNEY

Out above the ocean blue
There lives a dream, of me and you
Night-time comes, yet we remain
Together, on this wondrous plane

Thoughts I feel, are far beyond
If only, there was a magical wand
To take us on a journey far
No aims to gain, a shooting star

A bird which flies, so much afield
Can reap its strength and come to yield
Upon the Earthly plane, within
No goals to achieve, no deadly sin

Lastly, I will always be
Proud to love and proud to see
The contrast, which we have become
Together now, our journey done.

V J Haynes

LESSONS IN LOVE

We came together on a sweet summer breeze,
By autumn I am down on my knees.
Bursting with love, but full of pain,
Oh, my love, will I see you again?
At first I was afraid of letting myself go,
Sad and bruised from a previous show,
But slowly I thawed and grew into you,
And oh, how swiftly, my love came to bloom.
But, as I opened up and let myself go,
You, in return, withdrew from the flow.
Why did you let me swim deeper and deeper,
Allow my love to ripen, become sweeter and sweeter?
True, time waits for no man,
But, a few months more would have strengthened
                                    our love and plans.
Dreams of the future and oh, so much more
All shattered by the man I adored.

Sharon Louise Martin

When You Lose The One You Love

Your heart is still beating, your lungs they still breathe,
your eyes are still seeing but your mind wants to grieve.
They say you'll get over it and in time you will heal,
yet your sorrow is so bad you feel the need to conceal.

Your eyes they are burning, your voice it sounds strange,
your nights they get longer, you have so much to arrange.
You never will forget them no matter how long,
because their memories are with you, God know they're so strong.

Please think of them often, and send them your thoughts,
ask them for guidance when you think all is lost.
Don't blame them for leaving, their time it was up
to move to a beautiful place full of love.

Their suffering is over, their pain it has gone
their tiredness has lifted, their love lingers on.
Your new home they are building, your new path they must lay,
they know in their hearts you'll be together some day.

Please take time to recover from the tiredness and pain,
for you will need all your strength when you meet them again.
Don't cause them more worries, don't cause them more pain;
look after your health and your family's domain.

Their smile is so strong now, their eyes are so bright,
they will always be with you from morning to night.
Yet when you're sad, just you be glad, for the time you spent together,
this will again relieve the pain when at last you're all together.

Patricia McBride

WITH LOVE TO YOU I WRITE THIS

With love to you I write this
And from my heart these words I say
Your love and understanding
Are what makes each brand new day

Your hand on mine, your gentle smile
From lips so soft and warm
Your eyes reflecting all that's good
All bring the sun each morn

My darling, life for me would end
Should you decide to leave
Without you standing at my side
Each day and night I'd grieve

So take and hold this love I give
Yes, hold it captive in your heart
And we'll walk life's road together
And know peace at each day's start.

Don Woods

GOODBYE MY LOVE

The rain will still fall down outside
Now all that is hurt is my pride
The sun will go on shining above
Tears in my heart of a broken love
I cannot bear the way you choose to live
I stand alone with no more to give
Maybe you will change
But I will not be around to see
I will go it alone, I need to be free
Goodbye, eyes of green, no more pain
But always and forever, the sun and the rain.

Karen Langridge

FOREVER YOURS

On a warm summer's evening, hand-in-hand
We strolled barefoot across the sand
Two people so much in love for all to see
Living our lives for each other, me for you, you for me

Whisperings of love, as we tenderly kiss
Lost in each other, moments of bliss
Eyes expressing our deep meaningful love
Silhouetted against the setting sun above

That evening you asked me to be your wife
To be yours forever for the rest of your life
I still treasure that evening, the moment I said 'I will'
Thirty years down life's path, I adore you still.

Maggy Copeland